The Taste of Your Music

Poems By

Sarah Mackey Kirby

OTHER TITLES BY IMPSPIRED

Earth Magicke –
by Margaret Royall

Periodic Stories -
By Jim Bates

Dreams of My Heart –
By Aminath Neena

The Blue, Red Lyrae
By Mehreen Ahmed

Shiloh Osheen –
By As Viewed by a Poet Protagonist

Lost in Thought –
By Charlie M. Zamarripa

Habits of Totem –
By Ivan Peledov

Sarah Mackey Kirby

Thank you, Mark, for your love. My parents, for your support of my writing, for showing me what it means to love books, and for being doers rather than passersby. My family, friends, and teachers for your encouragement.

This book is for my sister, Robin.

Sarah Mackey Kirby

Acknowledgements

Special thanks to: Mrs. Gleason, the most supportive teacher a ten-year-old could have. Editor Steve Cawte *(Impspired),* for your patience and good person-ness. Pat Allison, for your gorgeous cover art and kindness. John Guzlowski, for your beautiful words. Carla, for showing up when it counts and being such a beautiful friend. LeaAnn, for laughs since those side ponytail, hair-catching-fire days.

Thanks to the publishers and editors who gave my voice space in your publications. *In order of poem appearance in this collection:*

Steve Cawte *(Impspired Magazine),* Laura van den Berg and Ladette Randolph *(Ploughshares),* Robin Stratton *(Boston Literary Magazine)*, Day Sibley and Shreya Tandel *(Dream Noir)*, Paul Brazill *(Punk Noir Magazine)*, James Penha *(The New Verse News),* Zvi A. Sesling *(Muddy River Poetry Review)*, Roderick Bates *(Rat's Ass Review),* Ginny Connors and Debbie Gilbert *(Connecticut River Review)*, Glen Phillips *(Front Porch Review)*, Madison Kalia *(Crêpe & Penn/CP Quarterly)*, Keith Sparks *(Open Skies Quarterly).*

- For the Love of Poets—*Impspired Magazine*
- Brain Basics—*Ploughshares*
- Good Evening, Death—*Boston Literary Magazine*
- A Quiet House—*Dream Noir*
- The Taste of Your Music—*Impspired Magazine*
- Boxing Nights—*Impspired Magazine*
- Ohio—*Punk Noir Magazine*

- A Woman in Tigray—*The New Verse News*
- Paddling by the Cave—*Muddy River Poetry Review*
- Cocktail Waitress—*Impspired Magazine*
- New Orleans—*Rat's Ass Review*
- Our Burdens—*Impspired Magazine*
- If I Could Run—*Impspired Magazine*
- Chicago—*Rat's Ass Review*
- Folded—*Punk Noir Magazine*
- You Keep Tellin' Me That—*Connecticut River Review*
- First Day—*Impspired Magazine*
- To Hell with My Brave—*Impspired Magazine*
- Those Old Steps—*Front Porch Review*
- Marrying You—*Rat's Ass Review*
- Where the Artists Hide—*Punk Noir Magazine*
- Dropping Blueberries—*Crêpe & Penn/CP Quarterly*
- Lost Umbrellas—*Open Skies Quarterly*

Contents

For the Love of Poets

I sat Paris café, Seine-faced,
strapped to a chair
meant for waste and cliché.
Among the artists. The poets.
The know-its. And dreamers.
All of us
sitting alone.

Where gathered
the thinkers, the fretters.
Do-betters.
Undiscovered no-namers.
The walk-of-shame lovers.
The talkers
sipping last night away.

The real. The irrational.
Referencing
green-leaf-arboreal.
Laying claim to mercurial,
mulling masterpiece
strokes with a pen.
Drinking in spin.
Folks of same vein.
This international blend
of chagrin
and insane.

11

Brain Basics

When you're in a helicopter with a
bleeding brain and the pilot reassures
you it's a beautiful night to fly,
it's hard to know whether to feel
relieved. I suppose that's better
than an iffy or a terrible night to fly.
Though isn't every night a terrible
night to fly with a bleeding brain.

And would dying in a helicopter be worse
than dying later in surgery. I suppose
it depends on whether the impact
would kill everybody instantly. Oh wait.
Everybody. The flight nurse, the paramedic,
the pilot. They'd die too. So I guess it's
best to have a beautiful night to fly,

for them anyway. But for you,
wouldn't together-dying be better.
Then again, even with people,
you die alone. Don't you.
Thought-rambles like that make for
good company while in a helicopter
with a bleeding brain on a
beautiful night to fly. Keeps all
actual dying away for a while.

Traveling Words

There is a place by the river rocks,
a place of dignity, a place of quiet.
Where I can still have breakfast with you.
Swallow the air, soothing as coffee.
Taste the moss of sweet cool oranges
dripping stains into the dirt.
Crisp toast tree bark, a backrest.
Where I remember all the days you loved me
and can wonder how to use the courage
you told me all the time I have.

Somewhere Along the Embarcadero

we bought Darjeeling
in a San Francisco tea shop.
Ate caprese flatbread on Fisherman's Wharf
in that place with all those pretty windows.
Speedboats and barges traveling
sun-soaked along the Bay.

Songs of lifeblood played.
Of seagulls flying over vessels
roped to their moorings.
Of cable cars harmonizing
with cold summer wind,
swishing fierce against our jackets.
T-shirts under layers if it warmed.
Our blond and brown locks intertwining
as we laughed through bird-squawk music.
Talking books. Talking school. Talking men.

I sleep in your t-shirt sometimes,
the one you wore that day.
And feel you wrap around me.
As sisters once did with arms
when gusts surprised us
on that West Coast August pier.
To hold each other up
when one was falling.

Good Evening, Death

Let it be tonight.
Okay, not tonight
exactly. Too much
to wrap up. But a night like this.
Star-covered and simple.
After Scrabble. No, not Scrabble.
No sense in giving him
a double whammy.
Chess or canasta,
so he can have the last win.

After cherry pie.
Because he'll have
gotten to sneak-watch me in the kitchen
and time his entrance
as I'm dough-covered,
struggling to reach more flour.
So he can walk over, lip pouted,
pat me on the head and say,
"Aww, I'll get it for you."
I'll give him my hands-on-hips,
pretend-offended stance.

On that kind of night.
Couch-curled, watching
one of the *Vacation* movies.
Or better, during George Carlin's

Flying on the Airlines standup bit.
Definitely not during
football. I don't want football
ruined for him forever.
And for me,
for obvious reasons…

But yes, watching something funny.
With the screen door
collecting nighttime
sounds. Crickets. Wind chimes.
Neighbors porch-talking.
Let the breeze feel chilly,
so I move closer to him.
Because I love his warmth
and need his coziness,
the relief that comes when
a car alarm stops screaming.

Help him remember his glasses
and the time I told
him to remarry
in case something ever,
well, you know…
I want him to have someone
to watch comedy with.
He forgets things.

And let me yawn
the try-to-stay-awake-but-
I-just-can't kind.
Blanket-wrapped
in his arms. Listening
to him crack up at the TV.
His laughter filling
the room as I drift away.

Sarah Mackey Kirby

A Quiet House

I decided when I grew up,
I'd have a quiet house.
Where snapping wind-tapped twigs
and magnolia leaves traced
an open window.

Where vitriol didn't
bleed through walls,
and slammed back doors
did not exist.
Where only eager barking dogs
could break no-loud-noise code.

Where tiptoed morning socks
would press against old oak slats
in perfect creak of settled floor.
Toward hush-baked kitchen's
hot coffee drips.

Where fear-shake voices
didn't upset nerves. And
sniffling noses stayed
reserved for colds.
Where yells accompanied
just good news.

A firefly porch where
summer tea ice moved
in a lemoned glass
as a porch swing drifted
through nighttime June.

Where Southern rain fell
fat drops of peace.
Where hearts never sped.
And quiet stairs led
to a cozy, laugh-messed bed.
Where dreams kept quiet too.

Sarah Mackey Kirby

The Great Conjunction

So comes the realigning.
Saturn and Jupiter crossing paths
on a winter solstice night. Some
pained anticipation that celestial rarity
means something deeper.

A need for righting,
for change in trajectory, so strong.
On earth, the dreamers dream.
The prayers pray. The hopers hope.
That the sky offers answers. And
peace will come. And this, the year
of hell can end. As the rereading
in Magi voices is heard again.

How spirits will be lifted with this belief.
Or disbelief. But for one night,
the planets will align. And faith
and logic will intertwine
in some space between.

Beach Morning

Those quiet few hours
before the splashing comes.
Before coolers and towels
lay scattered below the scorching.

When flecks of pomegranate
stretch into lavender. And salt
traces stacks of morning sand.
The foam feels different
during moon's fade
into the sunrise.

The water having night before
collected its batch
of Georgia Loggerheads.
Those that survived their
post-hatch journey.
In turtle-scurry
Bach-legato-soothing.
Movements under darkness of Divine.

Where air traces skin
in spiritual rekindling.
In sandal-hold-walk
foaming hope through ticking.
Seagulls flopping grace
against the awe.

With gold-flecked glow
smearing the horizon.
Where ships toss nets into the magic,
and surreal becomes poetic.
Where troubles tether
anchor-deep-to-ocean,
weathered into morning's
thankful calm.

The Taste of Your Music

I saw your heart
beatbox to clocks.
Tick Saturday night
in San Francisco.
You, sipping pale ale. Me, bourbon
on rocks. Your yuck-face
at first taste of sourdough bread.
Love pouring out of pores
onto table and wood floor.
Uneven meter,
smiling frantic-manic-sad.

I smelled your style
through Georgia blues
and summer's guile.
Your mellow saxophone
pecan-sugar laugh
wafting through salt air.
While people stared.
Dancing I-don't-care crazy.
Fingers snapping pralines on the street,
circling to the car.

I felt your voice
sing-song rhythm and reason,
winding through morning Chelsea.
Vibrating through pain's treason.

Timbre and texture
blowing in my ear.
Its varied dynamics
humming New York cheesecake.
Timid to crescendo
of spinning year.

I heard you plod
on Kentucky concrete.
Upbeat crepe myrtle
in magnolia neighborhoods.
Hiding stomps in tiptoes.
Your too-alone tone.
Scuffing shoes under constellations.
Dropping tears with no harmony
at failure to suspend disbelief.
No relief from joy's thief.

I tasted your pain
in Salem, Oregon's wind.
Standing on the cusp of sane.
Crevices of Corvallis stings
and a myriad of things.
Melody that went unchallenged.
Coffee-bitter quiet
before the rain
set in to wash you away.
Without giving me a say.

Boxing Nights

Only time you prayed.
Some profanity juxtaposed
next to Jesus.
Coz those were nights "shit"
could be said in front of kids.
And pool hall attitude
could lounge in the living room.

Fight nights hiding your gentle.
Half off your chair
leaning you'll-hurt-your-eyes
close to the TV.
Still smelling of backyard cigar,
lit brick patio, watching
stars break through the sky.

Peanut-shells-drop-carpet times.
White hair wrapping your neck,
annoyed your own cough
cut off the announcers.
Brooklyn boy cracks
shaking out the years.

Knockout-watch nights.
Left hooks and jabs grabbing hold
of your guts and that usually
settled tongue sprung free. Those

25

"Everybody-shut-the-hell-up" hours.
Bells ringing and you standing
yelling through the countdowns.

How you let me sit on the floor
next to you.
Coz during our no-nonsense
chess matches and morning walks,
you'd given me the heads up
about which "sons-uh-bitches"
had it coming that night.
Only granddaughters could sit close.

Ohio

I measure time between us in trucks
and tree-lurking deer on the side of I-71.
Because two hours and twenty minutes
are easier to swallow counting potholes
and county lines, guiding the way from
landmark to landmark. From McDonalds
to gas station to faded sign for the last
Kentucky rest stop before the bridge.
And I calculate the distance between us
in cell signal drops and time stretches
with good songs on the radio.

150 miles isn't far. But it's too far.
And how much I miss you weighs more
the closer I get, past every sweep of violets
scattered wild throughout the heartbreak.
And a river's symbolism changes
depending on the direction I go.
How North means a deep breath
before a sunlit Cincinnati skyline.
And I start to feel your arms gather me up,
knowing you're just another hour
from that traffic-patterned hill
curving teeth into the music.

A Woman in Tigray

is filled with stones,
nails. By her captors.
If she is not human,
if she must be bloodline-cleansed
from existence,
then why does crying matter.

The sun rises all over the world
as if it doesn't know.
And sets apricot embers
each evening.
In darkness, a woman in Tigray
is filled with stones.
Filled with soldiers.
Alone below Orion's belt,
sharp in the night sky,
glowing fire
three stars in a row.

*(The ethnic cleansing in the Tigray region of Ethiopia
includes gang rape and violence against countless women
by Eritrean and Ethiopian soldiers.)*

It Feels Like Cavatina

Choking you. Drowning you
in Beethoven's tears. This slow
depletion. How a heart leaks
until one day, its work is done.
How sparkling midnight fades into
winter morning gray. And every scalpel
that cuts flesh deep to give you hope
dulls useless. Piled on a heap
of medical waste. And needles
that puncture pleading skin
disappear into a sharps container.
How time swallows the pulse that rises
and falls on ECG machines, while friends
take their kids to see giraffes at the zoo.

And you are alone. With I-love-you
flowers that smell less each time
like going home. And more and more
of an afternoon eulogy.
Those kinds of thoughts.
Remembering days in Savannah
and nights in Chicago.
A Cavatina string quartet. That kind of sad.
That kind of calcified breaking.
Where if you don't smile hard enough
to hide the hurt, you'll crumble.

You will crumble.
Into an ancient piece of Mayan pottery
no one should have touched.
Into grains of sand blown into the ocean.
Into Picasso-fractured dreams
of untangling Christmas lights
and wanting more chances to ask him
why he throws wet towels on the bed.
Of grading papers, and parent phone calls,
and Friday night ice swirls while
some local band plays.
How every year means losing two.
And each hour hurries up the stopping.
Where pencils turn your tired heart to music.
A composition left to lure the night,
of a woman that some once knew.

God Writes Misery in Iambic Pentameter

I.
The lyrics soften all those specks of fright.
The pain, the salt that motivates the fight.

II.
Because factories close,
food lines lengthen,
and tempers blossom as fault lines.
Weeds along the trail become poems,
stilted words where hurt resides in guts,
and shoes trek through dirt-laced green.

In Kentucky's Appalachian wind,
the old dulcimer carries modern struggle
through strummed music. Where hands
grip morning coffee mugs as smoke
signals of folks refusing to sit quietly.

And in the cold Brooklyn nights,
the corner grocery illuminates the sidewalk,
conveying hope beneath a starless February sky,
that one day, other stores will light again.
And the subway cars will once more be filled
with commuters traveling hazy-eyed to work.

How ponderosa pines grow thick
dreams of forest, folding Oregon

in its branches. Serenading worried men
and crying women sorting through
medical bills, stacks of frustration spread
on the carpet before a two-dog audience.
How they still show tenderness,
that twenty-year kind of love
that hard hasn't broken.

Where algae stains
glow the Chicago River, as families
play cards and watch old comedies
inside walk-up apartments,
waiting for a coral-clouded dawn.

III.
Because the struggles penned are poetry,
the God-scrawled misery that tempts a fall.
The people turn their backs. To sing new hymns.

A Salty Senryu

While in the ocean,
a Box Jellyfish hugged me.
Everyone loves me.

Paddling by the Cave

It was that day canoeing
by Mammoth Cave. Two girlfriends
plunging oars into Green River current.
The air rife with April and
afternoon weed. Boys sneaky
and eager to share, to cement
foreshadow, their hope-drenched
return on a doobie-ous investment
we had no plan to pay back.

And oh how we laughed.
Drinking in the quiet last moments
before responsibility went viral
and a decade of weekend sleepovers,
tear-spectacle overreactions,
and leaning against oak bark,
legs stretched into twin pairs of sandals
slithered away.

That scorching spring day as we
floated through soft rapids, rocks
small and day calm. But still
the thrill felt real.
Too naïve to hurt yet.
Transition's tranquility
masking cliché of last hurrah.
Before the years melted
and the sting of needing you set in.

Cocktail Waitress

Years ago, back in the day,
slingin' them drinks
and smilin' for pay.
Upping my dumb in a sleek hotel bar,
conceding my brain
to a numb avatar.
Had to laugh sweetly
while your eyes fired lust.
How you knew you could treat me
while I hid my disgust.

Aww, bless your heart.
Ain't you a smooth talker?
Thought you could grab me
'cause you drink Johnnie Walker
Blue. Yeah you.
The you who'd spew out loud crass.
The thicker the wallet,
the bigger the ass.

Oh Derby was special.
The highest high-rollers
strolled in drippin' lavish
with jacket-flung shoulders.
Sippin' those glasses.
Knockin' off socks.
With a twist of dry wit.
Dipshit on rocks.

Cloud of illusions. Infusion of airs.
Smoke-laden breath
where corners wrought scared.
But more tips came in
if I drew out my drawl.
Deflated my dignity.
Inflated my "y'all"
'til last call.

'Cause tuition ain't free.
Sick isn't cheap.
And crying could wait
'til trying to sleep.

We Love For Real

We love active-verb-real.
That real. As rain creates
mud. Sloshing boots.
Stuck. Heads-together.
No words for the hard
or the stumbles. For the pain-filled
where-did-God-go days.

You? Getting through college?
Let's be honest. I might've
made it a tad easier
with my paper markup magic
when I didn't know
what you were trying to convey
or even what you wrote.
So you'd play video games and say
fix it up any way that sounds good, baby.
And I did. We love for real.

Through all those you'd-hold-me-
when-they-told-me-I-might-die days.
My couldn't talk, or walk, or
hide-from-the-clock.
The rocks through the march.
Years and years of it.
2013. That's some PTSD-forget-that-shit.
And I would PRAY. I would pray.

Those prayers were answered
by you getting cancer eight months later.
Not enough cuss words
for how fucked up that was.
But we love for real.

We love in the dark.
In the dirt.
In the shame.
In the my-skull-is-attached-to-a-drain.
Where wildflowers bleed into the horizon.
Where weeds foreshadow the dying.
Through the poison. The frightened.
The left-to-the-stars-to-fight-it.
We love in bleak. We love in mess.
In the blessed. It's our poetry.
It's how we love. For real.

Wet Leaves

Fall leaves gleam brightest
when wrapped in rain.
Wet and stacked,
shining red and gold.
Protected from shoe stomping
and crackle jumping,
in alluring piles.

Not victimized
by readied, smiling faces.
Untouched.
Except from chilly drops of morning.
When everyone steps aside
to avoid their squishiness.

Alone on the ground
or clasped to a tree branch.
Unbroken.
Sopping up calm
before sun disturbs their trajectory.

New Orleans

In deep nighttime NewAhLeuns,
behind a rain-dripping window,
a second first time.
Somewhere conflating the smells
of bourbon and wisteria.
Talking trombone in April's chicory wind.
Where gasps for breath under unmovable weight,
soul-wrought sobs in lonesome tone,
and unanswered prayers for stronger knees
at last floated to irrelevancy.
With you, they fell a natural, quiet fall.
The irony.

For such a place of drunken streets
and smoke-filled corners near Jackson Square.
Steeped in sin without the sorry.
To release and renew.
No haunted mirrors reflecting worthless ugly
or folded hands yielding empty.

Where different tears could form.
These, salty-sweet and welcome,
dropped from my closing eyes
as your patient fingertips pressed.
Caressed never-clotted wounds
that yearned to heal.
Garnering trust.

And squeezed pillow.
A respite found in every feel.

Where startled sighs and caring clutch
took hold.
In arms that guided, loved, and held.
Not stole.
Metered out in beat-drawn breath
that hadn't exhaled for far too long.
In cadence I could finally own.
The texture of safety
and quelled hate of an encased-me
who stayed out of reach.

A reprieve from years of off-key cries,
unharmonized, never-answered whys.
Forgiven by your confident tongue
that steered through my self-conscious shy
and moved with understanding.
Where wrapped soft cotton
hid sheets of self-blame.
And shame. And dearth of self-worth.
Confirmed with each touch,
this man wasn't the same.

The alleviation of fears
amid lips against forehead.
A reassuring *it's okay*.
And skin-swept overcame.
Far from forever-broken Sundays

and the need to double-check doors.
Turned from cruel betrayal of Holy Grace.
Stained the stars. Guitar-strummed,
hummed out fretted sane.
Logic breaking free from languished pain.
Untangling anguished mind
through rhythmic, midnight jazz
and every tear-traced vein.
As you tenderly filled the space inside me.
And I pieced together melody
a note at a time.

Where Unearths the Light

Like how one letter
transforms work to worn.
Screams changes quickly to dreams.
And laughter
when desecrated with an *s*
turns to slaughter.
How knees used for praying
can be knees used for killing.
And shadows become apparent
when light outlines their presence.

How constellations take shape
when stars have enough dark
to reveal their patterns.
And loves changes to loved
sometimes as time passes.
How heart moves effortlessly
to heard. Alone to atone.
Flee to free. Hole to hope.

How beauty unearths from the ground
as blossoms rise from dirt.
And humanity burns deepest
when humans give hands
to humans scorched.
To humans who hurt.

Sarah Mackey Kirby

Our Burdens

When I bake,
it's the best lemon cake you've tasted.
That ought to make me smile.
And my poetry. The next Emily.
You nod through every word,
even as you scratch your head.

Because blood clot mornings
and brain bleed afternoons
weren't supposed to happen.
Not to me.
And you understand.
You. Understand.
Dreams curl like thread
wrapping a spool.
How watching me hurts you.

So every fold in your clothes,
I crease perfectly.
Every coffee cup placement,
I space-plan strategically.
I am Monet landscaping Giverny
when I paint rocks.
Possess the greenest thumb
ever to grow dill.
Wear a sexy silk dress
in sweats and holed socks.
You're determined to convince me.

The Taste of Your Music

You. Must make up for it all.
For my plans. Sea-sunk
to bottom sand. Your pained eyes
shine endless encouragement
as you lift this burden.
Shoulder my off-balance drift.
How the weight of that. On you.
Is the heaviest I carry.

45

Ghosts Wear Sneakers on the L Train

Those old banshees, tired of traditional
haunting, take refuge in subway cars.
Slipping unnoticed through the turn-style.
Riding rails like city Woody Guthries
whose land stretches from Midtown
all the way to Brooklyn on the L train.

They wear just-bought Nikes, so it looks
like somebody left their shoes behind
for no discernable reason. Then, when
somebody walks over and reaches for them,
they raise them in the air, just for kicks.
Freaking the hell out of all the passengers,
who will go home and tell their families
they saw sneakers levitate.

And when the train screeches as it slows,
the ghosts stand and head toward the door.
And everybody lets them because eight
pairs of shoes that walk by themselves
don't happen every day. And the tourists
sit in awe by the absurdity. Their mothers'
words ear-ringing, suspicions confirmed.
That that's the type of stuff
that happens in New York.

Of Toothbrushes and Men

It's not the kind of infraction
that should warrant horror.
As you watch him. Brushing
his teeth. And can clearly see
a purple handle coming from
his hold-brush fist. It's yours
of course. Doesn't deserve the
about-to-come reaction or
to-your-core pissed.
But you walk toward him
and quiz him about
what color his toothbrush is.
And he says, "Green."

When you point to the one still in the cup
and you ask, "So what color is this?"
"Oh, my bad."
It's his ain't-a-big-deal nonchalance
about it that makes you madder.
Because next to purple, green isn't close.
And using someone else's toothbrush,
whoever they are, is gross.
Then, when he says, "Does it really
matter that much to start the day like this?"
And you say, "Yes, the hell it does!"
Because you'd stubbed your toe on a box
you'd asked him to move like three days ago.

And you were just then in the middle
of sweeping up coffee grounds you'd
dropped all over the floor. So toothbrush
sovereignty just became a cause worth fighting for.

And your brain cells fill with
all the stored-up stuff you've
mouth-shut ignored. But this feels like
a real good time to remind him of
every one of those. The back-pocket
transgressions and menial tension-fraught
should-know-by-now lessons. In the event the
need should arise to list them in
a long, no-pause diatribe. As he stares
at you like you're crazy. And you
feel crazy as you're itemizing.
Then he hugs you with his jaw on the floor,
causing your tears to start streaming.
Because he knows you well enough
to know the bottled-up-real-hard stuff
is what it's truly about.
But it all pours out that morning.
And to him, no less. All that stress
spilled from in-your-head rehearsals.
With down-hill-careen, let-it-fly passion
over the minor-but-really-it's-not
infraction of purple versus green.

Famous

If I were famous, I wonder
if I'd become a trendsetter.
Would women around the world
wear kangaroo pocket hoodies
to store their lip balm and phones?

And wear their hair wild. Not in that
took-two-hours-to-get-the-perfect-
curly-mess look. But in an actual mess.

Would muddy snow boots become the new stilettos?
Stubbled, vein-sprawled thighs the new tanned legs?
Chocolate chip cookie weight
the new smokin' hot abs?

I wonder if I'd advertise my mornings
with a hashtag.
Like "Woke up at four again." #InsomniaSucks.
And women everywhere would reset their alarms.

Sarah Mackey Kirby

Goodbye Grammar Hammer

Dear lexicon, syntax,
and yes you, semantics.
I'm done with your rules,
your despotic antics.
Ain't romantic to act frantic
'bout which words to choose.
When all I want is to write the blues.
And batting eyes—I love yous.
So screw you,
yeah YOU.

It's pathetic—I said it!
To have frenetic phonetics
'cause I'm here to explore,
not confound you with headaches
'bout the right "your" to use.
Lest the grammar hammer
busts down my door.
Cool your damn heels
on the floor.
There's no crisis.
Just a touch of poetic license,
of not quite the right words
in my repertoire. No permanent scar.
Promise, I won't go two, to, too far.
Allow some leeway. Okay?
Yeah. It's okay.
For real. You're gonna be okay.

I don't need comma drama
or flying sparks
'bout limiting exclamation marks.
Don't drool out your cryptic rules,
or go friggin' ballistic
over how I should adhere
to your sentence logistics
'cause I'm throwing down rhymes
while you're trippin' linguistics.
And I'm doing just fine.
Spittin' sublime.
Spilling my heart
while you freak
'bout which the right part of speech is.

Beseech me to use the right tense.
Wince 'til I choose,
and I know you're obsessive.
But that's some concern
we need a little bit less of.
Identify past vs. past progressive?
To be honest, most folks
don't know what that is.
And they still write their fights
on the pages they live.

So that horrid passive voice.
Dangling modifiers.
They're my desire. My choice.
Ending sentences with prepositions.

Pay attention. It's my contention
that if you wish to end with "in"
do it. Let 'em throw a fit.
I dare ya.
We're writers and poets,
and we're here to scare ya.
Make you think with ink.
A lil bit. Wink. Wink.

If I Could Run

If only for one day,
I could run.
Marathon distance or quick sprints
through the streets from my dreams.
No longer trapped
by this born-slowed-down heart.
Sewn up and seamed,
each beat out-of-step.

Feel a freedom, a redemption.
Unkempt hair blowing
dark, tangled mess.
In steady paces as lungs fill
with tree-blessed, wind-blown breath.
Tracing deep patterned time.
Embracing laced feet through uphill
climb, drum-pressing concrete.

Aria Sparrow. Violin wren.
Cardinal concerto.
Rustled-leaf-penned
orchestral accompaniment
playing bone marrow Zen.
Singing drizzled rain
that mixes with welcome sweat.

Gazelle-leapt steps of liberty.
No longer subject to
blood and brain
that won't behave.
Without constraints
or feigning brave.
If only for one day.

Southern Summer—A Sonnet

Where sweet magnolias effortlessly bloomed,
and wind could not slow humid summer sweat,
you saw me dance in late-night July room
and laughed a laugh that I could not forget.

The wicked sun bled rays unrepentant.
And moonlit hearts at last succumbed to melt.
Where wildest dreams held became ascendant,
the tributaries to the love we felt.

Through many years of life's tattered muddle,
where love's neurosis calmed to quiet ways.
The sexy sky bowed to gracious subtle,
unlike beginning's manic early days.

But on occasion, when you smile at me,
that early beat creeps up, and we fly free.

A Mountain Made of Concrete Blocks

stood gray-cloud high as we walked home.
My brother's eyes locked on the wall,
widening sea-storm blue. Affixed
and calculating options.
An impulse too wild for logic.
A force too strong to tame.
Not in that boys-will-be-boys way
like jump down stairs to break-arm fate.
Something more was there.

This, his snow-topped Andean peak,
at seven-years-old.
His down-the-road Himalayan ridge,
icy wind pushing against
a harnessed chest and
fingertip-clutched stone.
A calling climb to somewhere new.
God-designed with him in mind,
to find his feet. And feel him breathe.
And set him free.

"Gimme your hand," he'd said.
With confidence.
So I did. Instinctively, he knew
how to scale, what to do. To keep me
from falling to the ground.
Wanting me to share in this,

his prologue to the moon.
So we climbed toward peace-dipped sky
as mountaintops across the world
were made to wait.
And rocks to feel his grip;
to hold him in theirs too.

Sarah Mackey Kirby

Anna's Peaches

Anna's peaches begin late spring.
They smell of roses, and you can
prove their juiciness
with a thumbprint you're not
supposed to make. Hers taste the best.
Two-napkin sweetest peaches
that make up for the rest of her.
Plain face, whisper voice, strange gait.
A real background-stayer Anna is.
Not a laughed-at lady,
just a don't-know-she's-there lady.
Except starting late May.
Because everybody comes for
Anna's peaches. When she gets
a few months of not being
not right. As long as
it's a good season.

Chicago

We walked that stretch of city river.
Algae-baked, stained lake clay teal.
Face-feel icy, wind-kicked blow
in heart-broke heal and love that showed.
And oh-so-very-January snow.

White drops falling down from air.
No-coat you acting I-don't-care.
My eyes shined my I-told-you-so,
while those frost-wet hands
gave you away.
So I lent you my pocket,
and you gave me a smile.
Winter-paired,
we strolled awhile.

The joy when you saw
my blister-hide gait.
Traipsing the blues in a feet-bruised state
in shoes I'd owned since '98,
you'd warned me that I shouldn't wear.
Their worn-down soles with holes to spare.

So no-coat you and old-shoes me
river-bank moved with a skyscraper view.
Showing off dumb in tongue-freeze breeze.
Mouth-numb walking in five degrees.

My street-hobble feet
and your one warm hand,
with grins pinned on
in Chicagoland.

How Can My Heart Be Failing

when I can still walk down
Bardstown Road, scorching
concrete warming my sandaled
feet. And can rock out
old school, sitting in traffic
in knuckle-tight-
steering-wheel-squeeze
singing nineties hits.
Hair swishing to the beat.
My who-cares-who-sees
attitude pushing through
rush hour dead-stop.

Can it be so?
Though I can still kiss him
in that twenty-something way.
Intense mode of whole-life-ahead-
but-live-for-today kind.
And when blessings show
as fingerprints on skin, October's
nighttime tenderness gifting
breath to catch the morning.

Because love feels alive
and ashes feel remote.
How can my heart be failing
when waves still slide to foam

and moments live in snapshots
tucked in mind-kept frames.
When lilac smells like lilac
and ice cream tastes the same.
When wind presses cheeks
amid sun's drips of wonderful.
How filling fast with angel dust,
outcast-smudged, this distance
haunts me. Because I just
can't be done. And some days
it hurts to dream.

If You Listen for Me

You'll hear my voice rise through the summer trees,
puffy white magnolia blossoms already fallen.
It's the same one from all those long sister
phone calls. Your Oregon and my Kentucky
meeting in some line of longitude.
It's quieter now.
A little less confident.
A little sadder.

And I'll listen for your voice too.
It's fading some,
but I'll know it when I hear it.
All butter sweet
and cut with laughs.
And we will harmonize
inside some hallowed space.

Stitched

I am walking Haute couture.
Stitched up, fixed up,
lined with velvet.
Plastic-skulled in culled velour.
Metal hearted. Tailor-made
and scalpel parted.
Fashionistas' drooled-at, carted.
High-price-tagged
and flagged for stealing.
Scarred and charred
and marked for dealing.
Chiffon-loved with open back.
Ain't nothin' 'bout me on-the-rack.
Polished spleen.
Bedazzled liver.
Paris housed and bow-delivered.
Catwalk-gliding, frump-gown frocked.
High-horse riding, blood-clot styling
Alcoholed
and non-slip-socked.
Hugged by satin, draped in silk.
Fashion-forward, primped, embroidered.
Fancy ilk and special ordered.

Folded

I found you folded
like worn sweats faded into
the Tuesday doldrums.
Succumbed to monotony
of a grapefruit-lodged gut
that never eased its tension.

Into feel-nothing-refuge
that patterned your mornings.
Counting days in iced tea sips
and commutes to work.
Gone to the protected place
of dryer-lost socks.
Waiting to be lifted
from mindless trips
to the garbage can.

Long past the shock
that rendered you collapsed.
Past the brine
that pooled from your chin
into the nighttime ether,
bleeding its darkened howls.

You were folded.
Left to weight-press echoes.
The way our story began…
The memory of a father's love
and how much it crushed his son.

Sarah Mackey Kirby

Catching Sunrise in the Bluegrass

Cold Kentucky mornings tongue-dawdle
like coffee just before it's burnt.
The sun slow to spray paint
the sky gold and low in eye-level sting.
Shining snow, crunching footprint deep
toward old barns covered in wood rot
that time somehow turned beautiful.

And the horses nod to winter's dazzle,
then trot to warm-up exercise.
In the only place on earth where
they're saddled with
Pegasus-borrowed wings
in graceful gallop
'til take-off to full fly.

And the wind sings crying mandolin,
strumming Alison Krauss winter music.
Where mountains bleed to hollers.
Where towns bleed to cities.
Thawing ice-sad hearts
with still-there dreams.
Those notes of hope in key of G.

The wildness breathes out nectarine,
surrounding clouds with lived-in song.
Before flurries dance their toe-trip steps
of mapped-out graceful fall.
Like all the folks wrapped in strong,
clinging ground that covers hard.

Is There a Place...

Where rivers hum
and acorns crack on dry noon dirt.
Relieved of words,
sings late fall wind.
Where twig-swept footpaths
never end. And sharp blue Spruce
swallow the surround.
Where breath in thoughts
resounds through chilly time.
And scant a sound can be heard,
save scampering pads on tine-dressed paws.
In sugar-throated birds.
And tousled leaves that hug the ground.
Where sun-blessed eyes
soak in the peace.
That clutches dreams
and composes nerves.

I Drew You

I drew you watching fins turn to legs.
Climbing a braided-hair tower.
Kissing me a refuge from a poisoned apple.
Crayon-coloring blue sky,
shapeshift clouds of all that could be.
A sun-smiley-face fortress
enclosing me in warmth
that fixed alone.

I didn't draw old team sweatshirts
or shoe tops lifting from rubber soles.
No coffee-table mail and tea glasses
creating no-coaster-wet circles.
Or strewn about basketball socks
effacing the air.

I didn't paint unfilled gas tanks
'til the light comes on.
Music-blasted ears.
Unending disputes over
how cold you turn the thermostat.

I never shaded milkshake contraband
you sneak into hospital rooms
because I ask you.
Or your arms ribbon-wrapping
this hard-to-pump heart while

you thumb-trace my hand.
No oven-mitt attacks while
I'm cooking. Late night
toes in ocean water, foamy
ankles kicking up another chapter.

I didn't watercolor your selective
listening but rapt attention
when I read you my poetry.
No impromptu songs bragging,
"I'm the king of canasta."
Or blanket-couch evenings
with shoulders designed
for leaning.

I drew glass slippers
that never would have fit.

You Keep Tellin' Me That

Like that first real night.
All bluesy and boozy.
Tiny table in a big ol' pub.
Fries-grubbed. Knees rubbed.
That smoke tizzy
left us kissy, kissy, kissy.
You hopin' that might
lead to busy, busy, busy.
All sins-y
in a squishy, twisty frenzy.

How you watched me walk
back to my chair
with a try-to-hide smile
and eyes-wide, play-it-off stare.
Ear-whispering sweet things.
Securin' some bonafide.
Amid alto sax sings
and ice-glide strings.

And that chill-bone December.
Streetlight-ember glowing snow,
shined down on us while you helped me
heel-boot-route down concrete stairs.
I swear, just yesterday.
Wasn't it yesterday?

71

Sarah Mackey Kirby

You knew then.
And I did too. Just didn't let on.
Sixteen years come and gone.
But you still know every punk song.
And off-key, crack-up-blow that blues.
In old-school-style, you eye-smile
when I walk into a room,
with my slower moves
and my beat-down grooves,
you still whisper, "....

First Day

The first day you're told you might die
is a lonely day.
Not in the condescending
we-all-will-one-day way.
Or the shake-your-head at the,
"I'm-gonna-pray-for-ya-
'cause-things-are-in-God's-hands" way.
But in the tangible, hug-those-you-love
and throw-out-embarrassing-stuff way.
Because soon
folks will be going through your things.

And if you're lucky,
you'll have someone with you
when you hear it.
To catch you at near knee-collapse.
Hand you a tissue.
Give you a chest to lean into.
And if you're luckier, you won't.
So you can spend the loneliness alone.
Instead of giving a comfort-them speech,
as the pain on their face is worse
than all the rest of it.

But sometimes a breath
accompanies that first day.
A tinge of hope in the quicksand.
Not because the sky hasn't darkened
to soon-to-storm clouds.
Or because watching friends
swirl beer bottles and front-porch-laugh
doesn't give you an ache
you're ashamed you feel.
But because you keep
having those first days.
Have for more than thirty years
spinning seasons with the earth.
And somehow,
you're still here.

Where You Are Tonight—A Sonnet

Below the charcoal clouds that move March sky,
in gusty current, this reclusive space
descends and tugs—our moments gone awry.
Reminders of how much I miss your face.

I feel the way you hug me, though alone.
I hear your voice in all its tones and shifts.
This comfy place could not feel less like home
as weeks pass by in sea-storm-guided drifts.

If you were here, we'd laugh in living room.
We'd stretch in our just-us adorned milieu.
Despite this hurt, the pears and cherries bloom.
Unmoved by quiet days sans rendezvous.

Though where you are tonight aches deep-core-blue,
it helps to know how much you miss me too.

Sarah Mackey Kirby

To Hell with My Brave

I was born backed into a corner.
Knocking jaws. Spit-cussing
beats. Eye-cast meet-cute
with my retreat. Violating
nature's law. Strut-humming
streets. Who am I
but the oopsy-daisy fruition-come
of God's lazy-day faux pas.

Jigsaw-pieced woman fleecing time.
Blowing kisses to hits.
Rug-swept ashes-to-dust,
begging please-you-must-forgive
in a hushed evening cry.
Committing the crime
of fighting to live. Scar-dressed,
acquiesced to the tear-smeared
appall that reaches rawest gut depth.
Each step a new cusp.
Cooking dinner
while rustling up
this fomented side-hustle
of my borrowed life's
strained breath.

Battered and bloodied. Muddied
and swollen. Sick of the sick
in each day that I've stolen.
And nights of this fight,
staving off the depraved.
When's it enough? To show I've atoned.
And for what? For not dying?
It's trying. I'm tired.
This sin that I own.
Done with this grip.
This unending
almost-tripped grave.
To hell with my brave.
Just leave me alone.

Corporate Buzzing

Are you pushing the envelope,
moving the needle,
hyping core values
so the boss folk sees ya.
Being a team player 'til five o'clock frees ya.
Touting what's scalable, salable, available.
Spouting, "Wow, incredible, unforgettable,
in the hypothetical…"
'til you feel like you're a Jezebel,
sucked in and stuck in a distressed,
messed-up hell of selling bull.

A spider's lair of flailing lingo,
winking 'Bingo'.
Burned out, churned out, turned out.
Faustian bargain of spewing jargon.
Listening to allocutions 'bout finding solutions
as those brain cells are starving
for meaning to sharpen.

Lots of thinking outside the box.
Brokering power hour after hour,
while tick tock, tick tock, goes that clock.
Feeling like a schmuck keeping ducks in a row,
vertically integrating and remaining in the know.
Analyzing the gradations of how to grow and spin it,
'til one day somebody says,
"Hey, can I speak to you for a minute?"

Why Does the Dark

Why does the dark
magnify the senses?
Warm, night quiet
revving neurotransmitters
signaling time to think.
To become spooked by wonder.
Is it the windows
that no longer show the outside?
But in a lamp-stained glow,
give only my reflection.

Kiss Me by the Water

Kiss me where the late day sky
layers us in yellow.
In steal-us gusts
from achy hold.
Wet foam feet,
heels deep-dug
to sand, turned salt-traced mud.
While to-discuss
and those you-musts, flood
as hurt retreats.

Fasten me with
your storm-safe grip.
Cotton dress
pressed in your clutch.
Balance me as summer
hair-mess drips,
fashioned with your
bye-stress touch.

Hold me where the waves slide in.
Fingers under chin.
Lift me to you while I stand
sunk on tippy toes.
Those care-who-knows
and we're-caught stares
drift beyond the ships.

Take away tomorrow's pain
in worry-disembark.
Palmetto breeze
'neath not-yet-dark.
Gathered sand and
arm-wrap-squeeze
that shows me we'll withstand.
Take my hand
as sugared peach
evening glow descends.
My headwind friend
and Love 'til end.
Kiss me by the water.

Those Old Steps

Will you walk with me
to those old steps?
Cracked and broken,
stripped of depth. In
concrete crumbles.

We used to sit here.
Bare feet moments.
Clanking ice in humid
breeze, sweet verbena
just in bloom. Royal purple
knighting Spring.
Laughing nothings,
as young girls do.

I can see your smile, your
necklace bell, dangling
memories in porch swing wind.
Sycamore shadowed afternoons.
I feel your rhythm
trace the earth.
Will you stay with me a while?

Sewn Chest

He gazed at her scar.
Squinting eyes. Tilting head.
Examining the crimson imprint,
stitched-together skin
over battered heart.
Sexy flown evening sky.

She, bowed head,
stared at her sparkle-painted
toes. Cranberry red
to match the occasion.
A tear traveled past
a pressed jaw, floor-bound.

"That's enough," she said.
Fastened her navy shirt
two buttons higher
than ever before.

He kissed her forehead.
Gathered dark curls
to ponytail, then released.
She wiped her eyes, staining
his football hoodie sleeve.

"What do you want for dinner?" she asked.
"I don't know. What do you want?"

Marrying You

Broken pieces of glass still sparkle
when the sun catches the right angle.
Even the tiniest shards. Gleaming, wanting
to be noticed. Specks of former selves
collapsed into quiet corners,
waiting to be swept up.

Most of the year, Dogwoods lose their bloom,
replaced by small green-leaf canopies. That hide.
Or stripped to bare branches. Without protection.
But for a blink of time in Southern spring,
blossom pink and white, daring to unfold.
As they should, full potential on display.

High tide moves salt and debris
onto hard-packed sand, pushing through
hesitance of worn-down ocean at other times of day.
Daring to trace reluctant space.
Wrapping shells in foam,
shells no longer vulnerable to picking.

Marrying you was no beginning,
or saying of vows, or making of plans.
It was another day with you, same as all those before.
Where we fell into arms, and mouth, and skin.
Stilling the noise. Blocking stumbles
caused by shadows,
where sun should pour light.

Where the Artists Hide

We strum knockouts and drum beatdowns
with hair-band-metal intensity,
sweating demons from our pores,
headbanging kisses of tragedy.

Lurk spit-covered and stomped on,
collecting cobwebs in the wood rot.
Spinning dreams and tossing out
poetry into an earless wasteland.

Open our mouths to sing Ave Maria
but muster only Gregorian chants
in monophonic tapestry of Hell.
Dripping cringe beneath our day jobs.

Hide in the grout lines,
photographing soap scum
and built-up streaks of mildew
disinfectant longs to kill.

We stand hopeful in the garden,
mixing palette paint for water lilies.
But somehow, canvas-slap Devoured-Son-absurdity
in shaky-hand Goya, tendered for the haunting.

We sit stoic-ignored in corners,
gauging pulses on our night watch.
Scribble gin-sexed, smoke haze thoughts,
penning gut-dredged monologues on napkins.

Pirouette into the clapping,
feigning grace through pointe-shoe-Giselle.
Toe blisters staining blood into the satin,
as we smile to conceal our screaming.

We splay thoughts that wake up nuance,
crying charred into the morning.
Offer words that walk the story.
We tithe wicked truth to angels.

Standing on a Prism

Aries hugs the night that tends
all its sparkled, shadowed glory.
I've been standing
where the rainbow bends.
Between the rims of indigo and violet,
where thoughts ascend,
piloting a hard-read story.
Seeking brave all day.
Concave above a steely cloud
where courage meets cliché.

On the haunted street of On-the-Cusp,
refracting light through dim.
Threading worries.
Needle-stitching wind,
with a smile as I pretend.

Tonight, I dream across the space
of time zone, ocean, earth.
Facing worth. Counting messes.
For tomorrow I shall
press for breath
and sketches of amends.
Gripping every prism hue.

Still writing this
as beat-down stains accrue.
Where I belong.
Divine, this strong.
Knuckle-on these veins.
This love.
These tired steps.
For you.

New Jersey

The terra cotta Red Knots
share your Shore.
Birds of a feather, as it goes.
My momma from New Jersey
who gives me no-joke hugs.
Tugs brackish tears.

Sand-in-toes cloaks the years.
But you can't make your tough
stay in New Jersey.
Pretty lady standing small
who gives me voice
to say my y'all.

I can read your worried eyes.
The books that shelve
those parts of you.
You grab my hand
through every blow.
'Cause mommas know.

These squalls
like angels winging snow
that stretch the space we share.
Your arms a scarf
that forms my sail.
They see your face

and wouldn't dare.
Warn storms that try
to break my breath,
with every brave that you have left
that first,
they'll have to take New Jersey.

Sparkle It Up

Today, I'm gonna sparkle it up.
Bedazzle my frazzle.
Put sass in my class.
Sizzle out my fizzled out.
Undizzy my busy
and bask in de-task.

Unflask my bottled-up.
Slow down my throttled-up.
Shew away and do away.
Say no-way to every fray.
It's my pick-up-my-sick-of
and drop-kick-to-curb day.

Rewire my tired.
Unbind my mind.
It's my hold-tight to all right,
say no to they-knows
and thumb nose at on-toes.
Rework my prose.
Wave hey-hey
to come-what-may,
brave day.
Today.

Peeled

During those new-us nights,
we dropped our layers
like peel-easy clementines
as we pressed against
rind-dressed walls.
Sorghum-thick shadowed blinds
seizing crescent-delivered glory.
Content to have no clue

about things like bills stacked
to sucker-punch a final blow.
Stitched up synapses
and biopsy mornings,
finger-pointing some past life
infraction with karma-come-laugh.
Our now-we-know
and what-was-gonna-be
skip rock flung
into collapsing twilight fade.

Not then.
Back when my cotton sundress
swished harmony with summer
leaf-sway chimes, and we
kept eyes on each other
as roots clung to ground.
Because none of that

mattered yet. Not as we
slipped into evenings.
Nuzzling todays
and tossing clock-hands
while we soaked in
earth's endless offerings.

So Says Vivaldi

Each Season strung on violins
that play a message. Subtle. Bold.
Has Autumn passed? Is it yet cold?
The ice-block-chill strings Winter air.
Oh wise Vivaldi, can you tell?
Is last Allegro's curtain call
summoning my bow.

So many times
the Springtime cherries dropped
too quickly to the earth
and turned to Summer's scorching bath
without so much as wrath of storm.
And maple leaves turned red to brown
staining crisp on readied ground.
But then as if to change your mind,
another movement's poetry
lay bare E Major's sound.

As did I, in kind.
So which concerto
have you composed for me this time?
As you tend to do.
Your sweetest smile
with wink of eye.
Sonnet bound to season new.
Reason hold-tight-close to you.

Or is the snow a vast, wild wind
with struggles paid,
where breath ascends.
And angels point to waiting clouds.
No serenade. My encore played.
Where music finally ends.

Sarah Mackey Kirby

The Day I Walked Again

Early July, no-one-watching day.
Vine-tomato window view.
No be-careful, hip-lean-sway.
All alone. I stood up small.
In will-I-fall, mind tripped cue.
I stepped. And I stepped
in closed-eye kind of breath.
Afternoon living room,
beyond almost-death.

Set that walker aside.
In tiptoe, then stride.
Balanced through prayers
and haunts of their stares
that saw me as not-me
and longed-to-again-be.
I picked up my feet
in found-that-old-snare-beat.

Gaunt and unpolished.
My own self astonished.
Screw-fate-acknowledged.
Brave-near-demolished.
The day I walked again.

A Mind Like Yours—A Sestina

Was dark outside when pain descended deep.
When salted wounds poured out in beating time.
And stars that lay in Galileo's keep
dimmed brightest twinkles to a softer kind.
Hushed blue November's everlasting sleep
in graceful deference to a gorgeous mind.

Your sadness hid inside your Euclid mind.
Still, joy and laughs and love ran midnight deep.
The pulse of frantic, manic disturbed sleep
slowed sometimes when the sad showed just in time.
Confusion you responded to in kind,
and reached for loved ones' offer of their keep.

In angles', shapes', and colors' brilliant keep,
you called me up, and never did I mind.
A song-bird soul sang sweetest of its kind.
The fight inside you, twisting you down deep.
Behind the broken clock of shattered time,
I ask the world to rouse me from pained sleep.

For effortlessly can a burden sleep
upon the giving in to shadow's keep.
'Twas I who was born crushed on borrowed time
in clouds of ever-raining heart and mind.
But you? The hurt from losing you cuts deep.
I'm left with remnants of the cruelest kind.

Not tempered by remembering the kind,
the why is never answered in my sleep.
You loved all those dug into life so deep.
Reminders of the you I couldn't keep.
The beauty of an algorithmic mind
lay bare in cheerfulness, then loss, then time.

Like Schubert's music, yours, unfinished time.
Where constellations weep their starry kind.
Behind a strong, but gentle genius mind,
where decrescendo falls to silent keep,
your truth of drifting to forever sleep,
it bleeds an anguished different kind of deep.

Untangled mind plays strings of Autumn time.
Not captured by deep, moonlit-tortured kind.
My troubled sleep. And you in peace's keep.

Don't Use Soul in Poetry

Don't use soul in poetry.
Even though Neruda did.
Even though he put every
word that describes that linger
of spirit trudging the depths
into an algorithm,
and soul popped out every time.
For you are not Neruda.

And don't write stars as shining.
Don't write stars at all.
Or hearts shattering. Minds wandering.
Trees treeing. Rivers rivering.
And don't you dare write about the moon.
For the moon is overwritten and should
remain a celestial delight
to make you feel delighted.
But don't write delighted either.
No one says it unless they are trying
to delectate you with fanciness.
Poetry in-the-knowers
know these things.

Never use big words.
No one is impressed with
your polysyllabicity. Or any
attempt to get cute with language.

Find another way to say love.
Like my aching innards
swirl at your sight.
Except don't write that.
It's very bad writing.

Don't compare love to summer
or describe yourself as melting.
And for crying out loud,
don't use idioms.
Love can never be sick
or juxtaposed with puppy.
And if you write juxtaposed,
you are a pretentious prick.
Also, alliteration is always
antithetical to gorgeousness.
And apropos of wanting
to incorporate apropos
somewhere in here, don't rhyme.
Never ever. You're better
than that.

In the Garden

Blue clematis trellis-vine morning.
Tripping over a garden hose
next to monkey-grass-plopped dog.
His tongue stretched
to drink in summer.
Place where peace
overtakes urgency.

Fingernails fill with dirt
in forget-me-spots.
Terra cotta sacraments.
Hummingbird purple salvia.
Bumblebee fuzz drops pollen
as blossom volunteers
quench with nectar.

Sun illuminates dill
and parsley, hugging worn pots.
Wooden bed pepper sprouts
marinate in honeysuckle gusts.
As thyme sprigs arrange bits of calm.
Gathering thoughts
before an otherwise difficult day.

Already

One year gone.
Wicked grace.
November.

Bye, my sis.
Damn this space.
I miss you.

Squeeze, some days,
my phone tight.
Almost dial.

Fog of night
feigns opaque.
Vile is love.

Can't-blunt-sword.
Breathe your laugh;
map your face.

Your mined voice
fills my head.
I walk on.

A 1954 Dodgers Afternoon

It was Ebbets Field excitement
waiting for Duke Snider.
And Jackie. And Campy.
Back when kings ground-spit
on Brooklyn-proud afternoons.
And a ticket,
around-a-buck-nose-bleed,
cost us only saved-up
Elsie coupon ice cream wrappers
for a glimpse of might
penetrating clouds.

And my dad and I,
poor guys from Coney Island,
lined up for that look.
Because somehow we knew
few days could match this.
Or feelings could parallel
that popcorn-mouth-shove,
lemonade-gulp intensity.
Where we would share
in greatness among men.
How much he loved
ten-year-old me could still believe
I'd grow up to be just like them.

Sarah Mackey Kirby

And how they'd know it too.
Because we'd soon go to that September
Surf Avenue Mardi Gras parade
where players let every kid
hold out old baseballs,
shoving to get signatures
of those one-year-hence
World Series winners.
And all I'd have was the back
of a piece of paper and
the hope one would notice me.
The drop-jaw-awe on my dad's face
when I was the only one
to get autographs from six.

Your Woman

Soft are my stars that melt
into your hands. As you battle
against gravity that's followed
you too long. I give you my core.
A steady grounding,
love-wrapped dwelling
for you to exhale.

I am your liaison.
Between the dreary gray
you've dipped traces into
and the sun's worn longing
for your attention. Calling you
to come back from the
awake deadness knotted
through your center.

I am your woman.
Your woman.
My pieces, my spaces.
Flawed but well-intended.
Honey-laced to catch
your hurts. Where warm
shadows moving
nighttime prayers
bear witness to
your resurrection.

Sarah Mackey Kirby

Inside the Earth

Inside the Earth, the people live
in towns, in cities, everywhere.
They numb the pain they can't forgive.
Their hearts bleed more than they can spare.

They drive to work. They walk to school.
They fight in wars. And say a prayer.
The smiles they beam conceal life's cruel,
those steal-breath days that tend to wear.

They cook their meals. They hug their dogs.
They mend the wounds in need of sewn.
Inside the Earth, the people slog;
with billions there, they feel alone.

Sign of the Saucer Magnolia

Blossoms unfolding
spring-come-pink.
Holding gaze through
sidewalk breeze.
Spill of daffodil
lining brick.
Southern call for
peace of breath.
Thoughts pour
morning-thick.

Early daze
that won't last long.
In Robin song where cherries
weep. Rays of mourning
adorn the earth.
Sunrise drips.
Calming worry. Slowing
hurry. Nature rousing
from its sleep.
Sweet rebirth
of worth and since.

Sarah Mackey Kirby

We Fell in Love in Georgia

I carry your touch
with shells in my pocket.
Beneath a navy salt-splashed sky.
Where uncaught breaks
lift with waves'
gravitational pull.

In corner table shadows,
swirling bourbon-dripped ice.
Where ankles tangle amid
gritty-voice blues backdrop.
Midnight mood slides
June's sultry lavender air,
thick with smooth French horn.

Nestled under curvaceous
live oak branch stretches.
Canopy-draped Spanish moss.
Knee-shaking, jasmine-kissed
spaces of Sherman's March,
as our worries float
to a sea of Hostas
lining the footpath.

In sticky breeze,
where gathering clouds
hover over passing years.

I still hear our slow-rhythm vows.
And I feel Georgia
trace the nape of my neck,
as you whisper to me
things will be okay.

Sarah Mackey Kirby

Dropping Blueberries

I stand contemplating the significance,
watching blueberries drop
to the kitchen floor.
Entire carton, now released.
Rolling like pool balls
from a perfect break.

An ominous signal
of soup-dribble lap.
Lipstick to trace pressed collar.
Feather to adorn my curls.
A green marker streak
to decorate my face
with no one mentioning it.
All day.

These happen-together things.
Pepper-teeth pairs
with squeezing shoes.
Lost keys with running late.
Bird-gift windshield with
stay-still traffic.

Worrisome foreshadow.
Historical reference.
Superstition shunning logic.
Or surface-simply-what-is.
Blueberries sprawling tile
as sun paints a morning window.

Where Seagulls Fly

Take me where the seagulls fly
and peach light shows a glimpse
of coming day.
Where sun-drenched waves
below an Eastern sky
slide thinning foam
toward sandy beach's way.
Take me where the pelicans catch fish
and dive the ocean's
salt-splashed morning depth.
Where worries slip away
with far out ships.
Where troubles drift
to tide-wind's intercept.

Lost Umbrellas

That August visit. Sisters gazing
silver-sewn-blessed water.
Sheen-bright glass in glow
of Puget Sound.
Pressing heads and hands
that found the other.
Basking current-calm
of far-from-home.

We didn't get to say goodbye.
Not even windblown kiss
from tears' fall sidewalk.
Or miss-you waves,
paved block of lost umbrellas.
Where we'd shared each other's
hopes through all those years.

You'd moved as far as
dreams would let you travel.
But carried should-forgets
tucked blue-zipped suitcase.
Mind sometimes stuck in state
of its unravel. Watching
ferries drift in sunshine haze.

The Taste of Your Music

I wish I could have
held on to you longer.
Reassured you things would be okay.
I suppose that come-from-place
of lost umbrellas
won't let those face-on storms
erase in arms.

Breathe-free wild
tasting marsh-paint shadow.
In the place you'd said
we'd go together.
Tightened grip to San Juan Island days.
You. Destined to forever
live in poems,
while I write you space
to calm in warm-drip rain.

About the Poet

Sarah Mackey Kirby grew up among magnolia trees and lightning bugs in Louisville, Kentucky. She holds an MA in Teaching and a BA in Political Science from the University of Louisville. Her work experience ranges from waiting tables, to working for an eye surgeon, to teaching history to middle and high school students.

Sarah finds poetry tucked under rocks and dangling from front porch swings. She loves to cook, read, and travel and feels grateful for the life she has. Sarah and her husband live in the now.

https://smkirby.com/

Made in the USA
Las Vegas, NV
08 July 2022

51266305R00063